WORLD WINDOWS

Solids, Liquids, and Gases

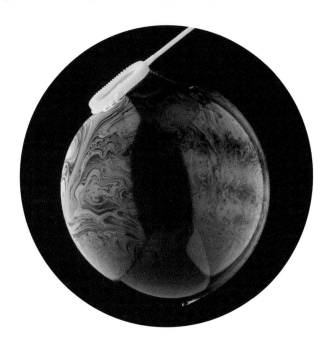

 HEINLE
CENGAGE Learning

Y|S|G
A YBM COMPANY
Young & Son
Global, Inc.

Contents

Vocabulary   4

Matter   6

Solids   8

Liquids   10

Gases   12

Summary   14

Fun Facts   15

Glossary and Index   16

matter

solid

liquid

gas

measure

mass

Matter

Everything around you is made of matter. Matter is anything that takes up space and has mass.

Mass is the amount of matter in an object.

There are three states of matter: solid, liquid, and gas.

The water is made of matter.

The air in the sky and inside the balloons is made of matter.

The grass is made of matter.

Solids

A solid takes up space and has mass.
Only a solid has its own shape.
It does not change shape.
You can measure the mass of a solid with a balance.
Crayons, scissors, and books are all solids.

You can measure the length of a solid with a ruler.

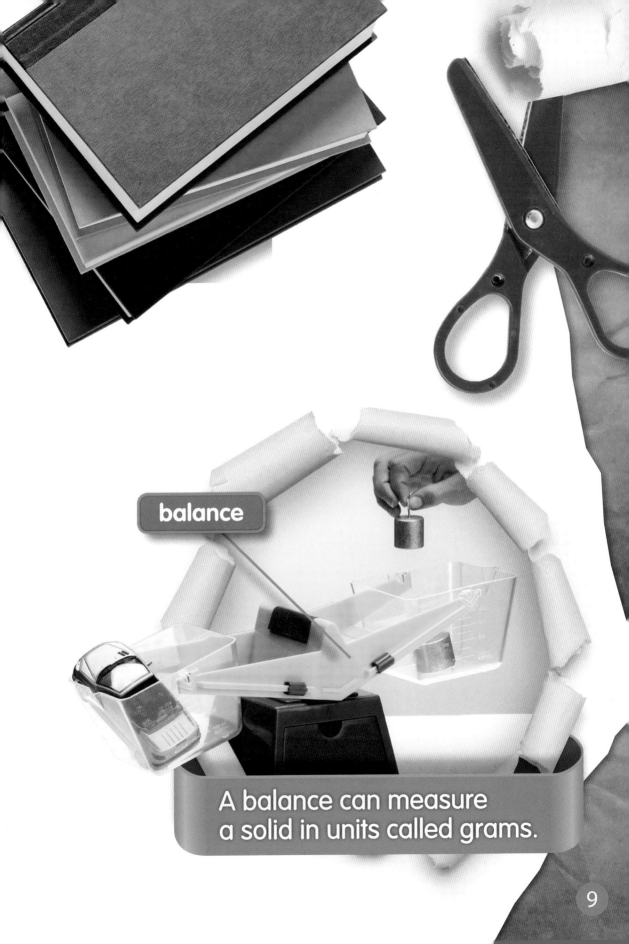

balance

A balance can measure
a solid in units called grams.

Liquids

A liquid takes up space and has mass, too.
Unlike a solid, it does not have its own shape.
It takes the shape of its container.
You can use a measuring cup to find out
how much space a liquid takes up.
Milk, juice, and water are all liquids.

Look at the different shape a liquid can take.

measuring cup

A measuring cup can measure a liquid in units called milliliters.

Gases

A gas also takes up space and has mass. Like a liquid, it does not have its own shape.

It spreads out to fill its container.

There are gases inside balls and balloons.

Gases also make up the air you breathe.

Bubbles are filled with gases.

You cannot see air,
but you can feel it. How?

Summary

What are these three states of matter?
How are they different?

Water Can Change

The water we drink is a liquid. But cooling and heating can make water change into a solid and a gas, too!

When water freezes, it becomes ice. Ice is a solid. When water boils, it becomes steam. Steam is a gas. When steam cools, it forms tiny drops of water. The water is a liquid again.

Glossary

breathe
To take air into and out of your lungs

mass
The amount of matter in an object

measure
To find out how long or how much something is

shape
The form of an object

space
An area that is empty or available

spread
To cover or open out over an area

state
The fact of being a liquid, solid, or gas

Index

balance, 8–9

like, 12

matter, 6–7

solid, 6, 8–10

takes up, 6, 8, 10, 12

container, 10, 12

liquid, 6, 10–12

measure, 8–9, 11

space, 6, 8, 10, 12

gas, 6, 12

mass, 6, 8, 10, 12

shape, 8, 10, 12

spreads, 12

unlike, 10